Write & Clean Hobbies

Om KIDZ
An imprint of Om Books International

Camera
Camera
Tripod
Tripod

Bird
Bird
Mountains
Mountains

Vase

Vase

Sketch Book

Sketch Book

Easel
Easel
Paints
Paints

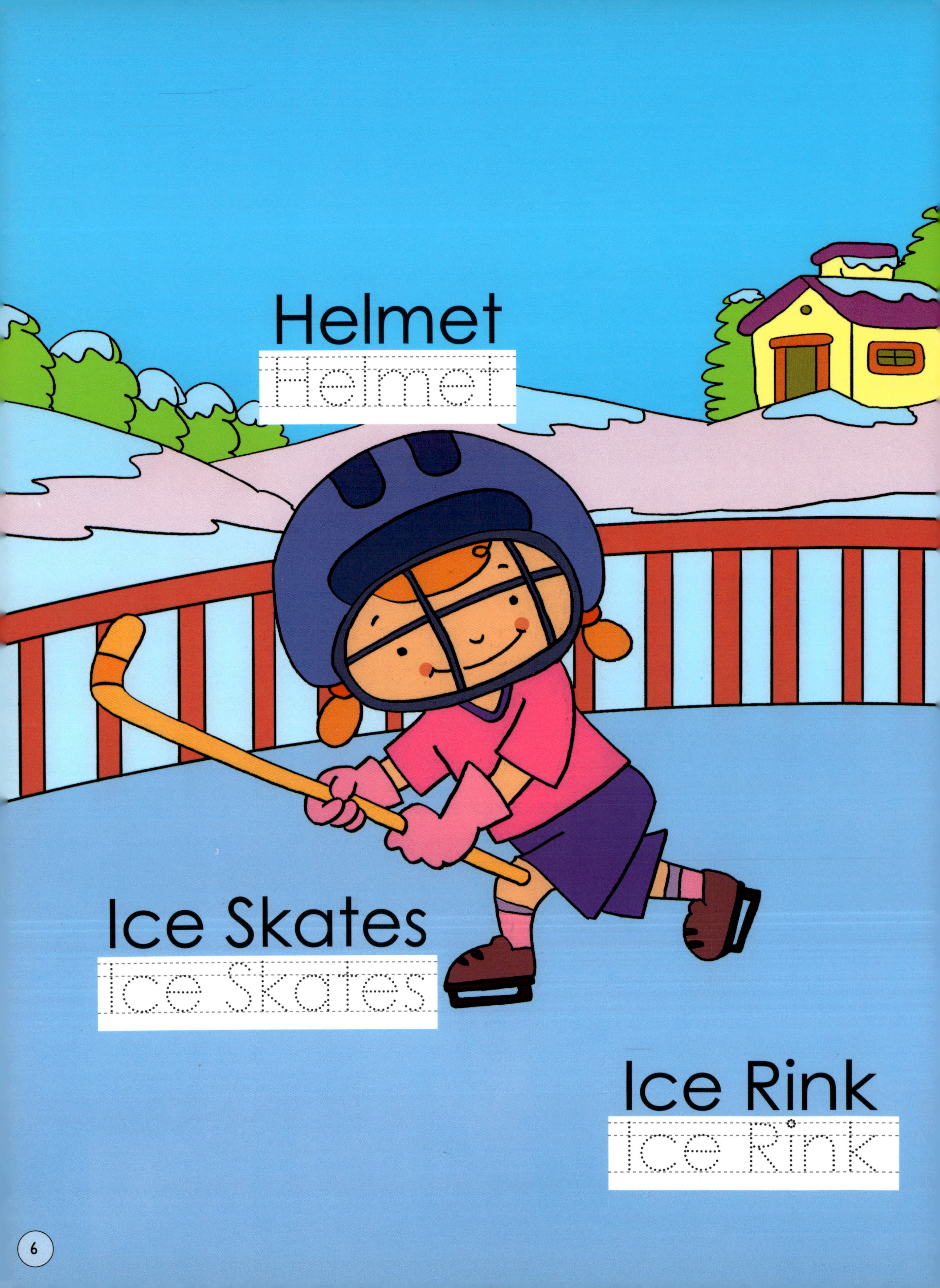
Helmet
Helmet
Ice Skates
Ice Skates
Ice Rink
Ice Rink

Puck

Puck

Moon
Moon

Stars

Stars

Telescope

Telescope

Bookshelves

Bookshelves

Books
Books
Librarian
Librarian

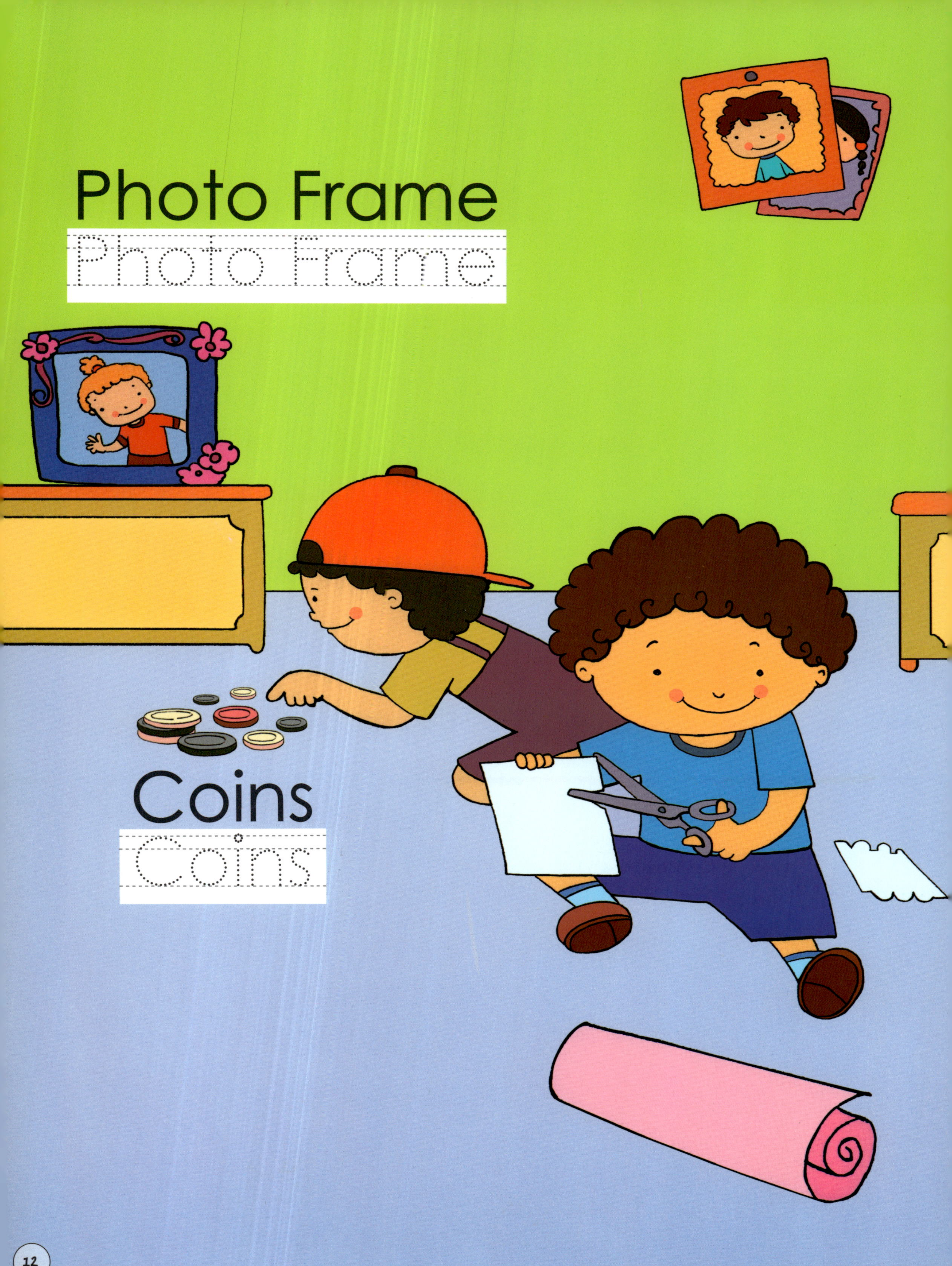
Photo Frame
Photo Frame
Coins
Coins

Glue

Glue

Scrapbook

Scrapbook

Match the following objects.

Camera

Puck

Glue

Telescope

Get to the ice hockey rink.

Published in 2017 by

Om KIDZ
An imprint of Om Books International

Corporate & Editorial Office
A 12, Sector 64, Noida 201 301
Uttar Pradesh, India
Phone: +91 120 477 4100
Email: editorial@ombooks.com
Website: www.ombooksinternational.com

Sales Office
107, Ansari Road, Darya Ganj, New Delhi 110 002, India
Phone: +91 11 4000 9000, 2326 3363, 2326 5303
Fax: +91 11 2327 8091
Email: sales@ombooks.com
Website: www.ombooks.com

ISBN: 978-93-84625-34-4

Printed in India

10 9 8 7 6 5 4 3 2 1